*To Bisho*

# MAN PROBLEMS

## *No More Broken Hearts*

*Rejecting Pain, Brokenness, and Bad
Relationships And Resolving Secret Issues*

*God has used you to
bless my life !*

### Rebecca Simmons

*Love you !*

*2-11-18*

Diligence Publishing Company
Bloomfield, New Jersey

The Scripture in this book is from various versions of the Bible including, the King James Version and the New International Version.

## MAN PROBLEMS

### *No More Broken Hearts*

### *Rejecting Pain, Brokenness, and Bad Relationships And Resolving Secret Issues*

To contact Rebecca Simmons to preach or speak at your church, organization, seminar or conference email: bhpministry@gmail.com

ISBN: 978-0-9963833-4-9
Printed in the United States

# TABLE OF CONTENTS

# DEDICATIONS

*Dedicated to Women everywhere. It is my prayer that the power and Glory of God be revealed and released through the pages of this book!*

This book is dedicated to my mother, Mae Thomas, who has been and continues to be my best example of what it is to be a strong woman of faith who continues to praise God in spite of everything that goes on around her.

I dedicate this book to my husband, Pastor Anthony Simmons, who walked with me and loved me in spite of my MAN Problems.

I dedicate this book in loving memory of my father, Ennis Thomas, who encouraged me to write my story and said he was looking forward to reading MAN Problems. I miss my dad and I thank God for restoring our relationship.

To my daughters Hakida Thomas and Kayla Simmons, my granddaughters, Niala, Sudani, and Niarobi Edmond and my spiritual niece, Erica Anderson. These young ladies exemplify courage, beauty, strength, intelligence, wisdom and faith. Their lives inspire me to keep moving forward and doing what I do.

To my sisters, Rasheedah Thomas, Jacki Bouie, Renee Jackson, Christie Morris, Vonda Thomas and Darlene Simmons. Also, to all of my aunts and nieces and female cousins, there are far too many to name.

In loving memory to my sister Janice Warden and my Aunt Geneva Bartley, who even after their lives have been lived here on earth continue to be two of my greatest inspirations.

To the women who cover, parent and mentor me spiritually, Pastor Dawn Tillery and Pastor Sharon Ryan, also to Pastor Phyllis Hilliard, Dr. Bernadette Glover, Dr. Denise Reid, Bishop Loretta Smith-Johnson, Joyce Meyer, Bishop Jacqueline McCullough, Dr. Kimberly Ray Gavin, Elder Lenore A. Artis, and the many more women in ministry who have greatly impacted my life. I am forever changed and grateful as a result of your pouring out into me and other women through your ministries.

Also, to all of the women who preach and teach the Gospel of Jesus Christ. Your courage and tenacity encourage me to keep going even when I feel like quitting.

Also, I dedicate this book to all of my spiritual daughters and the women of New Creation Christian Ministries including the prayer line.

Finally, this book is dedicated to women everywhere! You are truly wonderfully and fearfully made! Walk in it!

*To God be the glory!*

# CHAPTER 1

## *Facing My Own Issues*

"Get out! Get out, and don't ever come back! Ever! I don't need you. You can just go! Now! I can do bad all by myself!" I screamed at the top of my lungs.

As my husband stood there looking at me with a hurt, confused look on his face, I was also trying to talk sense to myself in my head.

*Girl, why are you doing this again? How many times are you going to try to push this good man away? Why are you acting so crazy?*

I shook myself loose from this sound reasoning. I didn't want to hear that. All I wanted to do was fight. I reached out and pushed him on the shoulder. "Why are you just standing there? Didn't I tell you to get out? Leave!" I yelled.

He grabbed my wrist and pulled me to him, chest to chest, face to face, eyeball to eyeball and breathed out these words, "I don't know what kind of men you've been dealing with out there, but I am not going to put my hands on you."

He paused and stared even harder into my eyes. The look on his face alone was enough to make me scared. Then he said, "I'm not going to put my hands on you. And you're definitely not going to put your hands on me."

He held me for a moment longer and then he let me go. No push. No shove. He just released me.

I felt so stupid and small. I felt pitiful and weak for trying to get this man who had vowed to love, cherish, and protect me for the rest of my life to put his hands on me and fight me!

"I'm...I'm sorry," I sputtered as he walked away and went up the stairs to our bedroom.

I was met with total silence. I had really messed up this time. I had pushed my man a little too far!

I had issues. I had problems. I had MAN. problems.

I had been Molested, Abandoned, and Neglected with everything else in between including being abused, lied to, cheated on, and rejected by men in my life, and it was interfering with my finding happiness in life. My whole life was impacted by what I had experienced, but especially my relationships with men.

In this book, I'm going to share some of the MAN problems that I had that led up to low self-esteem, abusive behaviors towards others and myself, and dysfunctional relationships with the wrong and even the right man. I hope that my transparency about my experiences and the wisdom that I have gained over the years will be like a reflection in a mirror for some of the issues that you personally deal with or have dealt with. You might even say "ouch" from time to time, but I encourage you to keep reading until you have read the whole book. It is time for us to face our issues and deal with the problems that prevent us from having great relationships, getting the drama out of our lives, having success in life and yes, even just receiving the love of a good man.

I know that I am not alone in the issues that held me back in the past. By the same token, you are not alone. Everybody has issues, and it's time for us as women to look at our own issues and deal with them! If we don't deal with them, they will continue to deal with us and wreak havoc in our lives. If we don't deal with our MAN problems, we will continue to be unhappy in life, love, and relationships. It's time to resolve the issues of the past and move forward to better!

# CHAPTER 2

## *Do You Have MAN Problems?*

D o you have MAN problems? Your actions may not be as dramatic as mine were, or maybe they are, but scenes like the one I outlined in the last chapter are an indication that something is wrong. If you are constantly pushing a good man away and being drawn into relationships with people who won't or can't treat you right, you could very well have MAN problems.

Ask yourself the following questions to begin identifying the problem:

1. Have you been <u>M</u>olested, <u>A</u>bandoned, or <u>N</u>eglected as a child or later in life?

2. Have you ever experienced being abused, lied to, cheated on, and rejected?

3. Are you having relationship problems?

4. Are you broken and burdened as a result of unresolved issues?

Because brokenness sometimes starts as early as childhood and can carry into woman-hood, it is my belief that this book needs to be read by every woman from every walk of life who has experienced any of the above at any point in their lives. God wants to tell you some things through this book and it doesn't matter to Him at this moment whether you go to church or not. It's a known fact that many people don't want to go to church because they think that the people in the church are hypocrites. I felt the same way. There was a time when I didn't go to church, and I would meet people who would invite me to church. I would tell them flat out that I don't go to church and that there's nothing in the church but a bunch of hypocrites. I later learned that some of what I said was true, but not all. I will share more of my testimony about that later.

Then you have a lot of women who walk into the church week after week with a heavy load and turn around after the service and carry that same heavy load back out with them. What is the purpose of that? I surely can't judge, because I did the same thing for many years.

It wasn't until I came face to face with myself and the issues that I was carrying and decided to do something about them that I was able to drop my bags and make some changes. I had to get sick and tired of hiding my pain, sick and tired of hurting, sick and tired of hiding from myself, sick and tired of being in denial that anything was wrong, and just plain old sick and tired of being sick and tired!

As women, before we can even begin to make the necessary steps towards resolving the issues in our lives, we have to:

1. Admit that we have issues.

2. Be sick and tired of being sick and tired.

3. Take the necessary steps to make the changes that will positively impact our lives and our relationships.

It's time out for dysfunctional relationships. You deserve the best in your life, and you deserve the best in your relationships. Someone once said, if you keep doing the same things you've been doing, you will keep getting the same results you've been getting.

It's time to say no to the same old actions and the same old results. It's time to move forward to take the necessary steps that will bring forth positive change and get you better results in life and especially in your love life!

# CHAPTER 3

## *It's Time For A Change*

*Come to me, all who are burdened and heavy laden and I will give you rest. (Matthew 11:28)*

It's time for a change. It's time to put your bags down. Whatever you are carrying in those bags, God wants you to hand them over to Him and leave them with Him. Don't pick them back up when you think He's not looking. God is always paying attention to what's going on in your life, and He is willing or should I say, He has already paid the price for whatever it is.

You may think that you're not good enough or that you deserve to live with dysfunction and drama in your life and in your relationships. You may even believe that you don't deserve to be happy or that life is as good as it's going to get. I can totally understand that. I've been there.

There were many years that I walked around with no self-esteem and felt that I was not worthy of the love of a good man. I had been through so much in life that I had believed the lies of the devil that things were not going to get better and that I would have to live with the pain of my past and the dysfunction in my relationships forever. But the devil is a liar! I thank God that I found out the truth and allowed God to heal me and give me a better life.

God's plans truly are better than our plans, and His timing is perfect.

I remember when God interrupted my life and my plans with His plans and brought change to my life through His divine timing.

I was sitting at home that night when the phone rang. I picked it up and my sister Jacki was on the other end.

"Hey girl, what are you doing?"

"Nothing," I told her. "Just chilling."

"Yeah right. You're probably sitting by the phone waiting for what's his name to call." She laughed.

I laughed only because she was telling the truth. I had been dating what's his name for over two years, and I could count on one hand the number of weekend nights that we had spent together. It was always the phone call during the week at about 9 or 10 o'clock at night when he would ask me in that smooth, sexy Nigerian accent, "What are you doing right now?"

And I would say, "Nothing."

He would ask, "So, are you coming over?"

With the blood pumping through my veins at the excitement of the thought of seeing him, I would say, "Yes, I'm on my way."

Then I would get in my car and drive over 20 minutes on the highway to get to my man to answer his call.

Jacki interrupted my thoughts and said, "You need to come out and have a drink. I'm at the Vanity Club. Come on over and let's hang out."

I said, "Okay. Let me get myself together. I'll be there."

I hung up the phone and jumped in the shower. I put on my short black skirt and a sexy black and white top with the shoulders out, put on my makeup, curled my hair and pulled it over to the side, put on my pumps and some perfume, grabbed my purse and car keys and headed for the club.

When I walked in, the place was packed. I scoped the room and spotted my sister near the back. I walked through the bar just like I always did, like I owned it. In my head, I was the queen of every spot that I stepped into. I was all of that and a bag of chips, some Starburst, Tictacs and a diet Coke. It was all about me, in my head, in the club, in the dim light, with the music pumping. This is who I had psyched myself up to be.

"How you doing?" this dude asked as I walked by him.

I glanced at him and quickly gave him the once over.

"Fine," I said as I kept moving quickly past him. I thought to myself. *Boy please! I will chew you up for dinner and spit you out for breakfast. How you feel like you can step to me and try to talk to me?*

Seriously, the dude looked like a total square!

"Hey Becky!" Jacki was waving and smiling brightly with that beautiful smile of hers.

"Hey sis," I said as I grabbed her and hugged her. "Hey Q," I said to her boyfriend at the time.

He spoke and Jacki and I made our way to the bar to order some drinks. I really felt like I needed to get some liquor in me to get this party started.

"Becky." I heard Q calling my name right after I gave the bartender my drink order. "I want to introduce you to my friend."

*"Oh, heck no!"* I thought as I turned and saw him standing there with the guy that I had spoken to earlier.

"Becky, this is Anthony. Anthony, this is Becky."

"Hi," the guy, whose name I now knew was Anthony said for the second time that night.

"Hi," I said as I turned my back to him to pay for my drink at the bar.

Jacki was sitting there watching the whole thing, laughing at me and cutting her eyes in the direction of Anthony.

"Is he still there?" I asked her.

She nodded her head. "Yep!"

"What is he doing?"

She laughed. "Nothing. He's just standing there."

"Should I turn around and talk to him?"

"Yeah," she said, "I think you should, because he sure is not moving."

I turned around and talked to him after taking a sip of my drink.

"Can I buy you a drink?" he asked.

I told him that I already had a drink.

"What you drinking?"

"Sex on the beach," I flirted with him. "Have you ever had it?"

Seriously square but tall, handsome, and chocolate, and I could have sworn I saw him blush as he answered, "No, I haven't."

"Well you should try it sometimes," I told him.

I looked over and saw my friend Big Ben come in the door. I got a little nervous because I knew that Ben claimed me when I was in that club. He was sure to come over and stand between me and Anthony and order me a drink from the bartender, and he did know what I liked to drink.

But then the strangest thing happened. Ben and his cousin, stopped at the table where the money to get in was collected, turned around and left the club. I know today that there were angels that turned them around and ushered them out of the club that night. I didn't see or speak to Ben again until almost a year later.

Anthony asked me to dance, and we hit the dance floor. I immediately noticed something different about him. Although he was a smooth dancer and had all of the right moves (which made me start to feel attracted to him), he did not dance with me like other guys. He didn't try to pull me up on him or grind on me from behind. He respected me, and I respected that!

After the bar closed, Anthony walked me to my car and invited me to church. Church! Wow! I shook my head thinking, *"Here we go. Another church going hypocrite."* I told him I didn't go to church. Then I told him what I told everybody that invited me to church. "I'm not going to church! There's nothing in the church but a bunch of hypocrites! If I'm going to Hell, I'll go from the barstool and not the church pew!" As I spoke, I looked him squarely in the eyes with a very serious expression on my face.

He told me, "That's fine. I like your spirit. I just want to keep in touch with you."

I was thinking, *"He likes my spirit? What kind of pick up line is that?"* Although I thought he was a little strange with that line, I gave him points for originality and gave him my business card thinking I was going to ignore his calls and try to find a way to get rid of him when he called.

I can only imagine what he was thinking. He was probably saying to himself, *"This girl needs Jesus!"*

I reminded him that I had a man as I got into my cherry red Beretta and started the engine.

He told me that was just fine because he liked talking to me and he wanted me to be his friend and not his woman.

That man ended up being my husband.

God already had a plan for me to meet my husband in the bar that night. He had a plan for me to stop sitting by the phone home alone on weekends. He had a plan for me to stop being a late night call for sex. He had a plan for me to be a wife. A Proverbs 31 woman!

God also has a plan for you!

You may think that you will never be able to get out of that bad relationship or that you will never find anyone who will love you like you need to be loved. You may feel like all men are dogs, liars, cheaters, or gay, and that there are no good men out there so you might as well settle for bad, but that is not true. You may be in a relationship with a man who will not commit to you like I was, or you may be dealing with a man who just wants you to be a side chick, or someone who wants you to just be someone that they have sex with and you're not even in talking status, but you don't have to settle for that. You may have been in one bad relationship after another and feel like giving up hope of ever being happy or married, or even if you're already married but things are sometimes not going that well, I am here to tell you that there is still hope.

Whatever you're going through in your relationships, marriage or life today I know that it is not by chance that you are reading this book. God is going to bring healing, restoration, and renewal to you in the area of your relationships! God is the God of the turnaround, and He is getting ready to do a new thing for you in the area of your love life. Married or single, this is your time for a turnaround. It's time for a change. Are you ready to receive it?

# CHAPTER 4

## *Molested, But God Had A Better Plan*

Due to experiences and circumstances in life, sometimes we as women just think we're not worthy of the love of a good man. When you have gone through a lot of MAN problems in life, you are prone to buy into the lie that you are not good enough, dirty, ruined, or damaged goods and that no good man will ever really love you.

Let me tell you a personal testimony about how unlovable I felt during the first seven years of my marriage.

It was early on a Monday morning and I was awakened by my husband of seven years sitting on the edge of the bed.

He leaned over and kissed me.

"I love you," he said as he stood up and headed out the door to go to work.

"You don't love me," I said, then I thought, *"Girl, what are you talking about?"* I (Rebecca) knew that Becky had shown up and was about to make trouble. I glanced over at the clock. 6:10 – He didn't have time for a confrontation. He had to

23

be at work by 6:30, and he was pushing it as far as the time was concerned.

Anthony turned around and walked back to the bed and sat down. "Why do you say that?" he asked me with care and concern in his voice.

"Because, I know you don't love me." I sounded crazy. "You don't love me. You don't know my greatest fear or my biggest hurt." I looked over and caught a glimpse of myself in the dresser mirror. I was morning ugly. My hair was all over my head, my eyes had a little sleep crust in them, and I had slept in an old t-shirt and sweats. Not pretty. Not sexy. Just a mess.

He reached his hand over to touch me on the leg and asked, "What is your biggest hurt and your greatest fear?"

I opened my mouth in amazement. I got ready to speak but before any words could come out, I heard the devil say, "Don't tell him! You have to keep that a secret. If you tell him, he's not going to love you anymore. He's not going to want you. He's going to leave you!"

"No! I'm telling!" I yelled at the devil and then I began to pour out my heart to my husband.

I told him about the time that I was molested as a child. I told him about the years of keeping it a secret. I told him how dirty and nasty it made me feel and how I never told anyone. I told him about the fear of being found out to be a fake and a phony. I told him about the hatred I felt towards the person who molested me. I told him about the pain of the memories and the anger that I felt. I told him everything.

Then I waited. By this time, I'm crying, and my nose is running, and I know I look a hot mess. I was sure this man was going to get up and leave that bedroom and leave me alone to deal with my shame, my tears, and my pain, but I didn't have to wait long to see that he was not going to leave.

He took me into his arms and held me tight and spoke these words into my ear, "I love you baby. I'm so sorry that you had to go through that. I love you so much, and I'm here for you."

He held me, and I cried. He held me until I stopped crying and then he said, "I got to go to work. I'll see you later, and I still love you!"

That morning was the beginning of a breakthrough for me. I had carried this secret for years, and I had never told anyone. Now it was all out, and the person that I told did not judge me or reject me. I felt so free!

The devil had been lying to me all along making me feel like the molestation was my fault, that I would be judged and blamed if I told anyone, and that I would be hated and rejected. The devil had held me hostage in a trap making me feel like I was worthless, dirty, and nasty because of what someone had done to me! The devil is a liar! God exposed the devil that morning for the liar that he is and set me free!

I felt like the woman with the issue of blood in the Bible who had been bleeding for 12 years. She was considered to be unclean because of her condition. She went to many doctors to try to heal her condition. Because of her condition, she was an outcast, and I could imagine what that did to her self-esteem. One day, she heard that Jesus was in town and that Jesus was healing people from all kinds of diseases. She probably said to herself. *"I've got to get to Jesus!"*

The Bible says that she said, "If I can just touch the hem of his garment, I know I'll be made whole."

So, at the risk of being stoned, laughed at, called names and talked about, she made her way to Jesus. She pressed her way through the crowd and touched His clothes! The Bible says that immediately Jesus felt power leave out of Him, and this woman immediately felt in her body that she was healed.

Jesus turned around and said, "Who touched me?"

His disciples probably had a good laugh about that one. "Master don't you see all these people crowded around you and you ask, who touched me?"

But Jesus persisted to know who had touched him, and the woman shivering and afraid finally came clean. I can hear her saying, "It was me Jesus! I touched you!"

I can imagine Jesus turning to look at her with love and concern in His eyes and saying, "What happened? Tell me. Why did you touch my clothes?"

The Bible says the woman told Jesus everything. She poured her heart out to Jesus, and after she finished telling Him about her issue that had brought her to the point of desperation to have her risk touching Him in her unclean condition, Jesus said to her, "Daughter, your faith has made you whole. Go in peace. You are healed of your disease." *(Mark 5:25-34)*

This day of telling my husband about all that had happened in my life was a day of breakthrough and turnaround for me. The secret was out! Now there was to be no more hiding. No more secrets. No more fear of what he would think of me or how he would feel if he knew what had happened to me, and no more being scared that he wouldn't love me if he knew I had been molested. This day was a day of the beginning of healing for me.

Yes, I had been molested, and it had held me hostage for over 30 years, but God had a better plan! You too, may have been molested or you may have gone through some other traumatic experience that really messed you up, but I am here to tell you today that it was not your fault and you do not have to live your life feeling devastated, guilty, afraid, or ashamed! I am here to tell you today that God has a better plan!

I don't know how long it's been, but today is the day of your breakthrough. Today is the day of your new beginning. As you keep reading, God is going to break shackles off of you and your life. The devil thought he had you, but God says no! God has a better plan, and He is about to manifest His plan of healing and wholeness in your life as He did in mine. That thing tried to break and destroy you, but you're an overcomer because of the mere fact that you're still here! You are more than a conqueror! You are victorious! Today is your day of victory! Today is your day of breakthrough!

# CHAPTER 5

## *God's Plan In Motion*

*For I know the plans I have for you saith the Lord. Plans to prosper you and not to harm you. A plan to give you a hope and a future. (Jeremiah 29:11)*

God began to orchestrate things so that I could complete my process of healing. I remember going to a women's conference at my old church where Dr. Gwendolyn Goldsby-Grant was speaking on the topic of *I Ain't Got Time For The Pain* which is also the title of one of her books. She had us all close our eyes and think about something that had happened to us that brought us shame and pain. Then she asked different women to come up and testify. I wanted to go up and testify that day, but I was too scared; so I sat and listened as other women went up to share their stories.

I sat with my mouth open and tears running down my face as woman after woman shared stories of how they had been molested – how they had been touched inappropriately, exposed to male and female private parts and subjected to all different forms of sexual abuse. They told how they had been exposed to pornography, alcohol and drugs, and molested by close family friends, family members, teachers, and even babysitters! There were also stories of women who had been neglected, rejected, abandoned, and physically abused while they were growing up.

As I listened, I felt the walls of shame begin to crumble as I realized that the devil had been lying to me all of these years in making me feel like I was the only one that some of these things had ever happened to. I felt a sense of relief in knowing that I was not alone; that this was not something that for some strange reason, had happened only to me.

Dr. Grant stood up after the testimonies and dropped a bombshell on the devil. She let us all know that what we had been hearing were stories of women who had been victims and that the actions that they had suffered at the hands of others were not their fault! What?!!! She told us that these acts had been imposed upon these women who testified and all of us who had similar testimonies. She told us that we were victims and that the molestation, the abuse, the abandonment, the betrayals, the rejection, and the rape was not our fault. Wow! I cannot explain the sense of relief and the wave of other emotions that hit me at that moment all at the same time.

I was in a state of shock that this had happened to so many others, anger at having been led to believe the lie that I was to blame for what had happened to me, and relief and joy at the discovery that it was not my fault. For so long, I had believed a lie, and on that day, I was exposed to the truth that set me free from the shame and the guilt. The molestation that happened in my childhood and the rape that happened years later, was not my fault! The rejection, the neglect, and the abandonment were not my fault!

Dr. Grant said that we were victims of an injustice, but that we did not have to live our lives as victims. She said that through the shed blood of Jesus Christ, we are victorious over what has happened to us in the past. She then went on to teach us that we had nothing to be ashamed of, and she helped us to release the anger by forgiving the people who had molested, abused, raped, rejected, neglected and yes, even abandoned us.

My God! So many of us were set free on that day! I felt the release of the shackles that had been holding me for decades. No more guilt! No more shame! No more believing the lies of the devil that I was dirty and not worthy of the love of a good man! No more chains! No more shackles holding me! I was finally free!

There is a real stronghold in the area of molestation because of the secrecy, guilt, and shame that follow the act. God wants to break the power of that stronghold for somebody today!

After being molested, I spent years thinking I was dirty, nasty, ugly, damaged goods, and guilty. Guess what? They were all lies!

If you were molested or had some negative experience that is making you feel dirty, inferior, small, guilty, undesirable, unlovable, nasty or ashamed, God wants you to know that you are not any of these things. You are not dirty, worthless, tainted, damaged goods, undesirable, nasty, unlovable, or any of those other negative things that you have been believing about yourself. The devil has been lying to you!

I shared my story with you to break the power of shame off of your life and so that you would know that you are not these things that the devil has been calling you. You are wonderfully and fearfully made, a woman of rare value, more precious than diamonds, pearls, and rubies, worthy of the love of a good man, and a blessing to the man who God has ordained to be your husband.

Specifically, in the case of molestation, you must realize that the molestation was not your fault. The person who touched you is the one to blame. You were not too pretty, too fast or seductive. You did not make them do it. You did not have on the wrong clothes or send the wrong signal. You were a child. It was not your fault.

You are not alone. You are not the only one that this has happened to. Statistics show that one out of every four girls, and one out of every six boys are molested by the time they are 18 years old, and it's probably more than that because many are like I was and don't tell.

Because of what happened to me as a child, I was very protective of my children in this area while they were growing up (although due to my drinking and other activities that I indulged in as a result of the molestation, I missed it with my firstborn and she too, went through her own trials with this issue), but once I sobered up and got my head on straight, I began to teach my children and grandchildren that if anyone touched them inappropriately or showed them their private parts or made them feel weird or dirty, that they should tell me. Because child molesters don't stop molesting, and because of the bondage affiliated with not telling, it's always best to tell somebody. I didn't tell because I was scared, but once I did tell I was able to move forward with my life.

Better is ahead of you. Your future is brighter than your past. You must begin to do the following things in order to get totally free from the negative experiences that hurt you in the past and move forward in victory:

1. Tell somebody what happened to you. Even if it was a long time ago. If you are still dealing with emotions and actions that stem from your being molested or hurt deeply in the past, you must tell someone. Talking about it will release you from the bondage of the shame and the guilt.

2. Give back the guilt. Remember it wasn't your fault. Place the blame where it belongs – on the person who molested or hurt you.

3. Forgive the person who molested or hurt you so you don't carry the anger and hurt around any longer.

4. Refuse to allow the experience to steal from your value. What happened to you does not make you less than. You are still valuable, precious, and beautiful.

5. Leave the past in the past. Move forward in faith knowing that God has a better plan for your life.

The devil's plan was to have you be molested or wounded in some deep way and to have that negative experience destroy you through devastation, anger, guilt, bitterness, shame, and unforgiveness that would carry over into all of the other areas of your life.

God's plan is that you would be victorious over every negative experience and move forward in faith to the great future that lies ahead of you. Yesterday is gone. Today is a brand new day. The worst is over. Better is coming! As a matter of fact, I would even go as far as to say better is here, and the best is yet to come!

# CHAPTER 6

## *Abandoned, Sexually Assaulted, And Taken For A Fool*

"It's over!" I heard my mother telling my father. "Leave now and don't ever come back!"

I stood frozen, hidden around the corner eavesdropping on their argument.

"You don't really want me to leave," I heard my father say.

"Yes, I do!" My mother's voice was filled with pain, but firm and serious.

I could tell that this time she meant it. The reality sunk into my young brain. My father was getting ready to leave and this time, he was not going to be allowed to come back.

There had been times in the past after my father came home from drinking with his friends, that he and my mom would argue and even fight. The next day or a week or so later, my mother would pack up her five kids, our clothes, and sometimes even get a moving truck and move our furniture and we would move to another part of town.

Each time, my dad would find us and talk my mother into taking him back. Because she loved him, she would give him another chance and then he would mess up again.

This cycle continued until one day when my mother decided she had enough! She was at the end of her rope. She was sick and tired of being sick and tired which had brought us to this day. This day was different. This day there would be no coming back. My dad had reached the end of his road with my mother, and their marriage was over.

My father packed up his bags and walked out the door. My mother watched him. I could see the pain in her face and the tears in her eyes that she refused to let fall.

I felt her pain, and I felt those same tears filling my own eyes as Daddy left the house.

He ended up moving across town somewhere and I think he eventually bought a house with his new girlfriend. I remember Mommy sending us over to the bar he owned to get money for school clothes and to have a visit with him.

One day I heard him jokingly saying to one of his friends, "Here come my kids. I know they need money for something."

He was only joking, but I was already hurting because he had moved out. I was already mad at him for leaving us, so I didn't think it was funny at all, and I never forgot hearing him say those words. I began to distance myself from my dad.

Mom would always tell us to go see him or to call him, but I wanted no part of that. I was so angry at him. All I wanted to do was live my life and forget about him like I felt he had forgotten about me. He tried to keep a relationship going with his kids. He eventually had another baby with his new girlfriend, and they lived in a nice house in the nice section of Newark. They called it the Weequahic section. After we had a house fire, we had to move into the projects in Newark, and my mom went on welfare for about a year. Then she got a day job, and then she got a night job and got off welfare. She moved us out of the projects to a nicer part of town. My mother worked hard to take care of her children, and I know I got my strength and work ethics from her. She was and still is a strong Black woman!

But as I watched Mom struggle, I grew more and more resentful towards my dad. I stopped going to see him and only went to his house when I absolutely had to. I felt abandoned by him, and I wanted to abandon him back. I felt like if he didn't want me, I didn't want him either. As a result of my feelings about being abandoned by my dad, I also felt rejected, unattractive, and unwanted or undesirable.

I began to act out and seek the attention of boys. If my dad didn't love me, I would prove that I was wanted by having every boy and man turn their heads in my direction. I went out looking for

37

attention. I started looking for love in all the wrong places. As a result, I woke up looking into some strange and even ugly faces! But that was not my intention. That was not the plan! As a matter of fact, it didn't even start out that way.

In the beginning years, after Dad left, I just felt like this ugly little lost and unwanted girl who had no father. There must have been some kind of look that I had about me that showed how lost, ugly, and unwanted I felt; there must have been some indication that I had no father to cover me because even though I was not looking for the attention from boys or men at this time, that is exactly what I got.

I remember being about 14 years old and, Dad had been out of the house about two years or so. I was a tall, skinny girl with kinky (now we call it coiled) hair that I wore in an afro (if you can call it that). I was coming home from school one day, and this older boy who was about 18 started talking to me.

"Hey girl," He flirted as he started walking beside me. "What's your name?"

"Becky," I said with my head down. I always walked and interacted with people with my head down in those days. I was scared of people. The old folks said I was scared of my own shadow.

"Where you going?" he asked.

"Home." I kept my head down. I kept walking.

"Wait," he said and grabbed my hand.

I tried to pull away, but he wouldn't let go of me.

He grabbed my wrist and held it tight.

"I'll walk with you," he said.

By now we were in the lobby of my building, and he pulled me past the elevators towards the stairs. I remember wondering where the people were. This was the projects, and there were always people around. Maybe there were people, but no one stopped this older boy from pulling me into the stairwell. We started walking up the stairs. Actually, he was pulling me up the stairs. He was still holding my wrist real tight, and I was scared.

When we got to the middle of the flight of stairs, he looked around to see if anyone was coming. Then he grabbed me and pulled me to him and kissed me. He pushed his tongue in my mouth and pushed himself up against me.

*"Eel! Nasty!"* I thought as I tried to pull away, but then he twisted my arm and kissed me harder.

Then he let me go, and I ran up the flights of stairs to the 6th floor where we lived. I banged on the door.

My mother opened the door and said, "Girl, what's wrong with you? Why you banging on the door like that?"

But I didn't tell her. That was my first mistake. I didn't tell.

This man-child waited for me after school every day and I would try to avoid him by going around to the other side of the building or taking longer to get home or finding someone to walk with me. But on the days that he caught me, there was always the twisting of the arm, the forcing of the tongue kiss, and the rubbing up against me.

Then things started to change, and I began to like the attention that he was paying me. This was my first kiss and my first boy paying attention to me. I started to look forward to our encounters in the stairwell.

Then things intensified. One night my mother and her friend went out to a party and left all of the kids at her friend's house.

"Lock the door," they told us. "And don't open it for nobody! Don't let nobody in this house!"

But me and my sister Janice, God bless her soul, and my friends were hardheaded. The boys, including this boy/man who had been messing with me, saw our mothers leave, and they came knocking on the door. We let them in. This young man who had been kissing on me and stuff took me into the bathroom and started his little game. Only this time, he took it further. I told him to stop, but he didn't stop. He forced himself upon me and took my virginity. I will never forget how much that hurt.

After he finished, he told me that I was his girlfriend, but that I couldn't tell nobody.

The next week, he told me to meet him at his house instead of going to school. I went to his house to have sex with him.

"Take off your clothes and get in the bed," he told me as he headed out of the room.

I took off my clothes and got under the covers in the bed.

Then he came in the room and picked up my clothes and left out of the room.

I remember thinking, *"Where is he going with my clothes?"*

Then his twin brother came in the room. I looked behind his brother and saw about three more guys. His brother started taking off his jeans.

"What are you doing?" I asked him.

"I'm taking off my clothes. I'm going to have sex with you. My brother said it was okay."

I was indignant! "No, you're not! I'm not having sex with you. I don't believe my boyfriend said you could!"

"He did and you are going to do it," he said.

"I'm not!" I yelled. I looked around the room and saw a woman's shoes and clothes in the closet. I thank God that I was really smart as a child (but obviously not smart enough not to be in this predicament).

"I'm not having sex with nobody!" I yelled. "You better bring me my clothes!" I kept talking. I knew I needed to keep talking. "If you don't bring me my clothes, I'm telling."

MAN PROBLEMS

"Who you gonna tell?" He looked amused.

"Your mother!" I said as I looked him directly in the eyes, and I wasn't laughing. I was not amused. "If you or any of those other boys touch me, I'm telling your mother." I could tell he didn't believe me, so I said, "As a matter of fact, if any of you touch me, if any of you have sex with me, I will not take a shower. I won't take a bath. I will stay in this bed until your mother comes home, and I will tell." I said it in as threatening of a way as I could.

"What if we throw you out?" he asked. I could tell he was getting frustrated with me.

"If you throw me out, I will sit naked in the hallway and wait for your momma to get home!" I was serious! Even at my young age, I had heard about gang rapes and sex trains, and I was not going to be the one that day!

He waved his hand at me and left the room. Not even a couple of minutes later, his brother came in and gave me my clothes. "Here! Get dressed and go," he told me. He looked angry.

I didn't care if he was angry. I was mad now. "No. As a matter of fact," I said, "I think I'll just stay here until your mother comes. I'm tired anyway. I think I'll just wait right here until she gets home."

"No no, you have to leave now," he stuttered. "My mother can't come home and find you here."

"I can't believe you did this to me!" I yelled at him. "I can't believe you were going to let all those

42

boys have sex with me. I'm supposed to be your girlfriend!"

He laughed. "Girl, you tripping. Get dressed and get out of my house."

I was hurt, mad, teed off, you name it. I got dressed and stomped out of that house.

That was the last time I interacted with him. No more chasing me home after school. No more catching me in the hallway. No more twisting my arm, no more kisses, no more grinding, no more trying to have sex with me. No more girlfriend on the down low. No more attention. No more nothing!

It was over for him that day, but it wasn't over for me. I ended up pregnant and losing the baby. Because of the void that was left in losing my baby, I ended up intentionally getting pregnant at 15 and becoming a mother at 16, but that's a whole nother story. I was so young, and I was making very adult decisions. Mine is just one story in a million of girls who have been abandoned and left uncovered by their dads. Mine is just one story out of the many girls who have had their virginity stolen when they told the boy no and he kept going. Mine is just one story of all of the girls who have been misled by some boy and set up to be gang raped or had a sex train run on them.

I was uncovered and ended up looking for love in all the wrong places. This was only the beginning. Now on top of the molestation, I had the added shame of the forced sex by this boy.

It's amazing. For years I told people that I had given my virginity away to this boy. Only in recent years have I come to face the realization that it was not a gift from me to him, but a theft. He took what I told him he could not have and stole my virginity. I want to stress the point of what I didn't realize for years and that is the fact that I told him no, and no will always mean no!

In spite of my telling this boy no, I did go willingly to his apartment to have sex with him after that, and I had to face the humiliation of the intended sex train. Now I had this shame along with the guilt of my early first teen pregnancy to add to the shame and guilt that I already felt from the molestation that had happened when I was younger and being forced to have sex with this guy. Emotionally, I was headed in the wrong direction like a derailed train that has lost control and is headed for a crash!

Just like molestation, those of us who have been sexually assaulted have to realize that it was not our fault. You may have been in the wrong place at the wrong time, drunk, with a very revealing outfit on or whatever; sexual assault is never your fault. No means no! If you tell someone no, they have to respect that and back off! So, if you have been a victim of someone having sex with you against your will or having someone touch you, molest you or sexually harass you, know today that it was not your fault; it was an assault against you, and you no longer have to carry the guilt or the shame of what happened to you. The person who commits sexual assault violates the rights and desires of the person they assault. You are not to blame for someone having sex with you against your will, molesting you, harassing you or sexually abusing you in any way. You were a victim, but you don't have to live your whole life being a victim. You can be set free.

On the following pages are steps that you can take to be set totally free from the guilt and shame of being in a situation where you were sexually abused, harassed or assaulted.'

**Steps to take to be set free (these steps can be applied to both molestation and sex that was against your will):**

1. Realize and accept that the molestation, non-consensual sex, harassment or sexual abuse was not your fault

2. Hold your head up. You have nothing to be guilty or ashamed about. You are not the only one this has ever happened to. Other women have gone through what you have gone through, and this is a crime that was committed against you.

45

3. Recognize that what occurred does not negate your value. You are still precious. You are still valuable. You are still wonderfully and fearfully made. You are still worthy to be married to a wonderful, respectable man who will treasure and respect you for the gift that you are.

4. Forgive the person who hurt you in order to free yourself from the bondage of anger, bitterness and pain. They don't deserve to be forgiven, but you deserve to be free. The longer you hold on to the anger, the longer the bitterness and pain will hold on to you. Let it go so it can let you go.

5. Move forward to better days. What happened is in the past. It's over now, and you can move forward to live the life God ordained you to live.

6. Tell somebody! Talk to somebody about what happened. Get help if you need it. Find a church, support group, pastor, therapist or friend that can help to walk you through your time of healing. Keep pushing until you get your breakthrough!

# CHAPTER 7

## Neglected, Unloved, And Rejected

I realize that while many women will be able to relate to being molested and abandoned, that is not everyone's story. So many women will stand up to testify that they were never molested or forced to have sex, that they were never abandoned by their dads and that they grew up in a home with both mother and father and none of these issues that I have written about so far relate to them.

But even in this group, there are a group of women who will say that their fathers were in the house, but they were absent emotionally. There's the woman who will say that even though her dad was there with her mom raising his kids, he didn't pay any attention to her. He didn't spend time with her. He didn't talk to her. He didn't affirm her and tell her that she was pretty. He didn't teach her about dating or help her to know how a man is supposed to treat a woman. She never saw him treat her mother with tenderness. He didn't bring home flowers or take her mom out on dates.

He went to work, he came home, maybe had a beer or two, watched tv, and pretty much ignored her. Or maybe he was a pastor, or a deacon in the church, and his whole life was consumed with other people. Or maybe he was just a hardworking man who didn't spend quality time with his kids.

This is not a judgement against a dad who falls into this category. There are many men who are great providers for their families, but do not know how to interact emotionally with their wives and daughters. I only bring up the dad in this category to highlight how important the role of a father is in the life of his daughter. Daughters who grow up without attention, affection, and affirmation from their fathers often end up with relationship issues later in life.

Those would be the women who would say, I was not molested. I was not sexually assaulted. I was not abandoned. I was neglected. I felt unloved. I felt rejected by my dad.

You may not only have been neglected by your dad, but you may have been neglected by your mom as well as a result of what was going on in her own life. I remember having the following conversation with my daughter when she was young:

"Mommy, please don't leave me," my daughter begged me as she grabbed ahold of my dress.

My heart broke as I looked at her little tear-streaked face.

"Kida, I have to go. I have to go to work baby."

"But I don't want you to go to work." She grabbed me around my legs and held on tightly.

I couldn't move. I reached down and tried to pry her little hands loose. "Baby, mommy has to go to work so that I can pay the bills." I explained to her. "If I don't pay the bills, we won't be able to live in this nice house and we will have to live in the streets."

"I don't care!" she said. "I'll live in the streets. I want you to stay home with me!"

"Now honey, you don't mean that." I guided her over to the couch, and we sat down. "You don't want to live in the streets. That's not good. Besides, I have to go to work to buy food and to buy you clothes."

"No!" She folded her arms in front of her chest. "I don't want you to leave. I don't want you to go to work."

After a while, I was able to convince her to let me drop her off at my mother's house and go to work for which I was already late.

I was upset that I had to be late for work again, but I certainly understood my daughter's dilemma. I was all she had and I had been home with her all of these years until she was five years old, and now I was leaving her every day to go to work. Not only was I going to work during the day, but sometimes at night I was leaving her with my mother so that I could go and hang out with my sister or with my friends or boyfriend. One thing

49

I tried not to do was expose her to different men, especially since I had broken up with the only father she had known (my ex-husband who had been in her life since she was a toddler).

Even though she kept a relationship going with him, inside I could tell it was not enough. She still had memories of her biological father and when she was 16 years old, she told me, "I want my father."

I told her, "You have your father." I was talking about my ex-husband.

But she told me, "No, I'm talking about my real father. I'm going to find my father."

I told her about her biological father's mother and where they lived, and she went on her search to find her father. She did find him when she was 21. He was in the hospital getting ready to pass on from this life. He had been asking for her and he held on long enough for her to come to him and visit him in the hospital. Shortly after that, he passed away.

I thank God that she found her father, but I regret the fact that she did not have a lifelong relationship with him. I never pushed him out of her life. Shortly after she was born, he went to jail for something stupid and I didn't wait for him. When he came out, I was married. He told me to get a divorce and marry him. I refused. We went our separate ways, and my daughter was neglected by both parents in the process of our individual methods of survival.

I have apologized and made peace with my daughter who is now a mother of four awesome children and has a testimony of her own, but in the process of me trying to grow up, I messed up and she had to go through a period of being cared for and taken care of, but still neglected.

I can't even begin to share her testimony and how that led to her looking for love in all the wrong places, dysfunctional relationships, a dysfunctional marriage, divorce and a season of searching for her own identity, but I can tell you that the neglect that she suffered as a child contributed greatly to the mistakes she made as an adolescent, a teenager, and ultimately as a woman.

We have all experienced neglect and even abandonment or rejection in some areas of our lives. It often starts close to our hearts with our absentee fathers or fathers who are not paying attention or are emotionally disconnected. This leads to feelings of abandonment and rejection and begins to eat away at our self-esteem. Then it extends into other areas of our lives, our platonic relationships, and ultimately, it plays out in our romantic relationships and our marriages.

If you were neglected by your father or mother as a child, a spirit of rejection has probably attached itself to you. In order to get free, you must realize that your parents are people too and that their neglect of you was no reflection of who you were or are as a person. You must realize that they were dealing with, or in most cases not dealing with, their own personal issues and in some cases, just trying to survive. Some fathers never received emotional affirmation while they were growing up. Some fathers never saw their fathers showing love and affection for their wives and children, so they did not even know where to begin showing love and affection to their own wives and children. Some fathers just figured it would be enough to pay the bills and protect and provide for their families, while others ran away and disconnected from their daughters (and even their sons) because the relationship with their wife or baby's mother had gone bad.

## Steps To Healing

1. In all of these cases, it is important for you to see that the blame lies with the father or the parent who neglected you and not with you. Again, we hear the five magic words "It was not your fault!" It was not your fault if you were neglected. The blame lies with the person who neglected you and not with you. It's not that you were not good enough, not pretty enough, or not smart enough. It's not that you were too dark, or too light, too skinny or too heavy, it's not that you were too ugly or too bad.

2. Acknowledge that the neglect that played out in your childhood was because your parent or parents had issues of his or her own that they were dealing with, forgive, and release him (or her)! You must see that truth, and you must forgive your father (or mother) for not paying enough attention to you or giving you what you needed emotionally. You must release them, so that you can release yourself to be whole and free from the effects of the neglect of your past and the spirit of rejection that may have attached itself to you.

3. Know and declare your value. From this point forward, when you feel yourself feeling rejected and left out, say to yourself:

"I am enough. I am not an outcast. I fit in where I belong, and if I am not accepted by someone, it is not a reflection of my self-worth. I will no longer live my life under a spirit of rejection or fear of not being accepted. I will no longer try to be what others want me to be just so I will fit in. I will no longer compromise myself or my values, and I will no longer play small just to make others like me or feel better about themselves. From this day forward, I declare, that I am valuable and I am enough!"

# CHAPTER 8

## *Choosing The Wrong Man To Love*

MAN problems can lead to us as women making the wrong choices when it comes to being in a relationship. As a result of being molested as a child by someone I loved and trusted, and feeling abandoned and neglected in my relationship with my father, I have entered into many dysfunctional relationships.

I have been in abusive relationships where I fought all of the time both verbally and physically. The crazy thing about it was that in my dysfunctional thinking, I actually thought that it was okay to fight the person that I was in relationship with. Oftentimes, the fights would get out of hand. I actually had to leave my ex-husband for good after a fight where I was on the floor and he was straddling me and holding me down because I was going crazy fighting him. He was so angry at me that he picked up a clothes iron and was about to bash me up aside of my head with it. I knew when I packed up my clothes to leave that day that I could never return.

I remember trying to run over one of my ex-boyfriends with my car because I saw him with another woman after I had left him for another man. It got so bad that my dysfunction became dysfunctional, and I got tired of fighting in my relationships. I wanted it to stop, but I didn't know how to stop it.

I remember having to put a restraining order out on one of my ex-boyfriends because he would not stop showing up and harassing me. He would show up at my apartment, my job, and even the places where I would go to hang out with my friends. He would threaten me and one time, he even grabbed me and tore my blouse as he wrestled with me trying to take the keys to my brand new car away from me. This man called me names and did everything he could to tear down my self-esteem that I was at this time just building up, but I thank God that it didn't work. I finally went downtown and put a restraining order out on him.

I remember being in court with him and the judge said to him, "This young lady says you're harassing her."

He said, "Your honor, I'm not harassing her. She's harassing me! I just want you to get that monkey off my back!"

The other people in the courtroom laughed. It was obvious that he had come to court high.

The judge looked sternly at him and said, "No, you're the monkey on her back, and I want you to

56

stay away from her. If you see her coming down the same side of the street as you, I want you to cross the street. If you even come within a few feet of her, I'm putting you in jail. Do you understand me?"

My ex-boyfriend's squinty eyes got so wide. "Yes sir, your honor," he said. "I understand. You won't have no problem with me."

I assumed he didn't want to go to jail. He was too pretty for that. Mr. Player had gotten played, but the game was over, and he had to leave this girl alone. Hallelujah! Thank you Jesus! I didn't have a relationship with God at that time, but God was watching over me!

I had been in an abusive relationship (both verbally and physically) with this man, and I was so happy to be out! No one deserves to be verbally or physically abused. We as women have to know that we are better than that and that we deserve better! There are many other kinds of relationship issues that result from MAN problems. If I wrote about all that I have been through in relationships, I would need ten books on this topic.

A popular side effect of MAN problems is being in relationship with the wrong man! Wow! How many of us can testify to that? How many times have we just flat out picked the wrong person to love? Let me tell you another story. This one's a shocker!

I was walking down the street one day when I was about 18 years old and my daughter was almost two. I ran into an old friend who was with a friend of his. I was immediately attracted to the confidence level of my friend's friend. He was well dressed. He had on shoes, slacks, and a nice shirt. This was unusual for the hood because normally the guys wore sweats or jeans and sneakers. My friend's friend smiled so bright it lit up the whole block and he spoke proper English with boldness. Well, we hit it off, exchanged numbers, talked on the phone a few times, and eventually started dating.

We dated for a while and then moved in together. The old folks would say we were shacking. One day, I decided to clean out the closets in our apartment. He was in the National Guards, and had these duffel bags in the closet. As I was moving the bags around organizing the closet, I noticed that one of the bags had a padlock on it.

"Why is this bag locked?" I asked myself out loud.

Now I'm curious, so I start patting and feeling on the bag. As I patted the top of the bag, I feel what feels like magazines.

*"Now I know this man don't have no dirty magazines in this bag,"* I'm thinking while at the same time trying to figure out how to get into the bag to find out what kind of magazines they are. My reasoning voice is saying, *"Well, you know he*

*likes to dress. Maybe it's GQ."* But I wasn't going to be satisfied until I got in that bag. So, I roll up the magazines and maneuver them through the hole that is on the top of the bag. I pull out the magazines, open them up to look at them, and my mouth flies open in total shock!

They are dirty magazines! But that's not the worst of it! They are magazines not of naked women, but of naked men with naked men! I slide down the wall onto the floor and begin to cry my eyes out. This is before the AIDS epidemic. This is before the gay pride revolution. No one was proud to be gay during this time.

Just then I heard the key in the door, and my boyfriend at the time comes in happily. "Hey Beck..." he says before he stops in his tracks at seeing me sitting there against the wall, outside the closet, crying. "What's wrong?" he asked me.

I picked up one of the magazines and threw it at him. "You're a homosexual!" I yelled at him. "You're gay!"

"No. No I'm not. I'm not gay," he said.

"Then what's this?" I hissed as I threw the other magazine at him. "What's this garbage? How can you being a man look at naked pictures of men with other men?"

"Beck. I don't even look at the pictures. I just read the stories. I'm telling you, I'm not gay! I just read the stories in these magazines. That's all."

I wanted to believe him, but as he tried to hold me, I pulled away from him. How could I be so dumb? How did I end up living with a man who's gay?!!!

Well, he stuck to his story and we stayed together for a little while longer, but one day when I was gathering dirty clothes to do the wash, I found pictures that he had cut out of the gay magazines tucked into his socks in his sneakers. Remember he said he didn't look at the pictures! Lies!!! He had real dirty laundry on top of his dirty secrets in the closet that he continually lied to me about. I never got what I believed to be the truth. We ended up breaking up and going our separate ways. The funny thing about it is that at one time, I wanted to be married to this man and have his children and spend the rest of my life with him.

As I look back, I know that he was never really into me. I was the one pushing for us to live together, to get married one day and to even have kids together. I was the one pushing for us to spend more time together when he would disappear for hours and even stay out all night claiming to have gotten high or drunk and fallen asleep at his cousin's house. I was the one denying the signs, and ignoring his best friend who told me that there were rumors of this man being gay. I was the one turning a blind eye and even believing every lie because I wanted to be loved by what I now know was a man who could never fully love me.

Denial of the truth is a harmful thing. I was devastated when I found those magazines and pictures. I didn't want my relationship to end, but I could have brought a lot more pain to myself had I continued to live in denial. I thank God that I woke up and moved out. I thank God that my days of being deceived finally came to an end. I believe that I was lied to, cheated on, and rejected in that relationship. I believe that this is an occurrence of MAN problems in adulthood caused by the MAN problems that I encountered in my childhood. One thing I do know for sure is that my MAN problems were causing problems and creating issues in my life. I was looking for love in all the wrong places and constantly picking one bad relationship after another!

I know that I am not the only woman who has ever chosen the wrong man to love. I know that I am not the only one who has found incriminating evidence against the man I was in a relationship with and continued to be in a relationship with that man. The truth of the matter is that many of us do this as women. We believe that the wrong man is the right man for us. We believe the lies in spite of seeing the truth with our own eyes. We believe that he will love us, that he will get a job, that he will commit to us, that he will marry us, that he will start telling the truth to us, that he will stop hitting us and being verbally abusive to us! We believe that he will change, and the truth of the matter is that there is a very high likelihood that he never will. The truth of the matter is that we have once again or even for the first time for some of us, chosen the wrong man to love!

This is a cycle that can and must be broken. You do not have to settle for less in your relationships. You do not have to be that friend with benefits, chick on the side (or side chick as the young people call it). You do not have to be his girl on the sneak tip or down low. You do not have to fight in your relationships or be verbally or physically abused. You do not have to tolerate being mistreated, lied to, deceived, cheated on, rejected, taken advantage of, taken for granted, or disrespected. You deserve better, and you can demand better.

I always tell the girls and women that I mentor that you teach a man how to treat you. I also tell them that a man will do no more to you than you let him get away with. If you set standards and put your foot down on how you will or will not be treated, that man (if he is worthy of being in your life) will pay attention and straighten up and do right by you. Open your eyes and look in the mirror. See your beauty. See your value. Write down a list of how you want to be treated in your relationship or marriage. Write down the type of man you will or will not date. What are the qualities and attributes that you want him to have? Be clear and be true to what you really desire for yourself in a relationship. Then, when the next man who wants to date you comes along, pull out your list and check to see if he fits the description of the type of man that you want to date and ultimately marry. If not, don't even waste your time. Haven't you been through enough emotionally by picking the wrong man to love in the past? There are some immediate, definite "no's" that we as women should set when it comes to who we will or will not spend our time with. Here are some of my suggestions and what I would use for my own life if I were single:

If he is already married or in a relationship, that's a no. If he wants to keep you a secret, that's a no. If he only calls you late at night and never on weekends, that's a no. If he never takes you on a real date, honey, that's a no. If you have to beg him to call you, pay attention to you or treat you right, uh, no! If he asks you for money, that's a no. If he does not have a job, need I say it? That's a no! If he is rude and/or gets angry fast, that's a no. If he shuts down and won't even talk to you for days after an argument, that's a no. If he won't commit to you and wants to be friends with benefits, heck no! If he ever puts his hands on you or calls you out of your name, that's a no – brother man has got to go! If he does not have a place to stay and wants to sleep on your couch in your apartment or worse yet, in your bed, that's another no. If he does not love and serve God, NO!

I have found that the reason my husband is so good to me is because he loves and is accountable to God. He fears God, so he has to treat me right! So many times, we date men who don't love and serve God and wonder why they don't know how to treat us. A man who will submit to God is submitted to the Word of God which tells that man to love his wife as he loves himself, even as Christ loves the church to the point where Christ laid down His life for the church *(Ephesians 5:25)*. A man who loves God will make his girlfriend his wife, and he will love his wife even to the point of laying down his life and wants to please her!

I have only listed some of the no's that will prevent you from falling in love with the wrong man. The key is to not even begin to date a guy who already falls beneath your standards of what you want in a relationship. Never open up your mind (or your body) to a man that you already know is not right for you. I always say, if he can get your mind, he can get your body and if he gets your body, he's got you, and it will be hard to break loose because then you will have created a soul tie! A soul tie is an emotional, physical, and spiritual bond created by sex that will keep you tied to a man even if he treats you bad, abuses you, cheats on you, or dumps you for another woman. Soul ties are very hard to break and can keep you tied to the wrong man for years!

It's time to break the cycle of choosing the wrong man to love. However, in order to do this and be totally successful, you must resolve any MAN problems that you have. Let's move to the next chapter and begin the process of resolving MAN problems.

# CHAPTER 9

## *Resolving MAN Problems*

MAN problems can lead to many issues in our lives. They include looking for love in all the wrong places, anger, resentment, low self-esteem, hopelessness, neediness, lack of ability to trust, dysfunctional relationships and marriages, being in relationship with the wrong man, lack of attraction to the opposite sex, homosexual behaviors, fear, drug use, alcohol abuse, abusive behaviors towards others or our children, inability to achieve measurable success in life and an overall urge to just throw in the towel, settle for less and not hope for anything better in life. This is not a psychological analysis, just an overall assessment from my life experience and the experiences of others that I have talked to.

You may have gone through a lot in life, but there's hope! What has happened to you or what you have gone through in life does not have to dictate to who you are today or your destiny for the future!

You are wonderfully and fearfully made. You were created with a purpose in mind in the heart and mind of God, and you don't have to live a life that is a result of problems that you have had in the past! You are not stuck. MAN problems can be resolved!

## 10 Steps to resolving MAN Problems

1. **Admit that you do have a problem** that is related to your being molested, abandoned, neglected, lied to, cheated on, rejected or abused, or hurt in the past.

2. **Affirm the fact that it's not your fault.** This is something that was done to you. You were a victim. You were not the cause for what happened. You were not too fast, too pretty, or too needy. You were not too ugly, too skinny, too fat, too dark, too light or too lacking in anything that the devil may be lying to you about. You did not bring this on yourself. You did not make the person molest you, sexually assault you, abandon you, abuse you, neglect you, lie to you, cheat on you, or reject you. It was not your fault. Put the blame on the person who is really at fault – the person who hurt you. That's where it belongs.

3. **Forgive the person or the people who hurt you.** You must forgive everyone involved in your MAN problems. You must forgive! If you are like me, you are probably thinking they

don't deserve to be forgiven or they didn't even ask to be forgiven, and you are right. Most of the people who have hurt you in the past do not deserve to be forgiven, nor do they ask for forgiveness in most cases. But let me offer this to you: They may not ask to be forgiven, and they probably don't deserve to be forgiven for what they did to you, but you deserve to be free. You deserve to be free from the bondage of having to carry anger and bitterness around with you. Forgiving them is not about them. It's about you. Not forgiving holds you hostage to the pain. Not forgiving holds you in bondage to your past. Forgiving sets you free! You must forgive them so that you can be free to move forward and leave the past in the past!

4. **Forgive yourself** for any wrong actions that you have taken as a result of your pain and as a result to what occurred in your life to make you act out in retaliation. For instance, not only was I looking for love in all the wrong places as I went from man to man, but I was also, looking to retaliate and make every man pay for what men in my past had done to me. I had it in the back of my mind that I was going to make every man pay for what others had done to me. This was dysfunctional and only hurt me and made matters worse for me. They were living life and going on about their merry business, but I was still living in the pain of

my past. I had to let it go by forgiving them and then I had to let go of the guilt and shame of my own actions by forgiving myself. I had to forgive myself for not being a good mother. I had to forgive myself for abusing alcohol and drugs. I had to forgive myself for being sexually promiscuous and mistreating men. I had to forgive myself for all of the wrong that I know I did as a result of the pain that had been inflicted on me by others. So many people forgive others, but they forget to forgive themselves and still don't get totally free from the problems and pain of the past. Once you have forgiven others, forgive yourself. Give yourself the precious gift of freedom through forgiveness of yourself as well as others.

5. **Forget what is behind.** Now when I say forget, I don't mean wipe your memory clean. As a matter of fact, you may never forget some of the things that have happened in your life even if you want to. What I am suggesting here is that you pay no mind to these things any longer. When painful memories try to come up in your mind and make you angry, pay no mind to them. Push them out of the forefront of your mind by thinking of better days already experienced and yet to come. You may even have to release fresh anger and pain of the memory by saying, I forgive that person for that again. I forgive them and they owe me

nothing. No apology. No explanation. Nothing. Take some deep breaths, pray, meditate on some scripture verses or something positive, or play or sing your favorite uplifting song.

6. **Press forward to what's ahead.** Yesterday truly did end last night. Today is a brand new day and tomorrow is filled with potential, promise, and possibilities! Set your mind on your dreams and your destiny. Guess what? The devil tried to stop you, but he lost! You are moving onwards and upwards to the life that God ordained for you to have. What is it that God has deposited in your heart to be, do, and have in this life? When you were a little girl, what did you want to be when you grew up? Focus on and press ahead to pursue your dreams.

7. **Put your faith in God for total healing and wholeness.** Earlier in this book, I talked about the story from the Bible of the sick woman with the issue of blood, and there is also a little girl who had died. When the woman heard that Jesus was coming through town, she was at the point of being sick and tired of being sick and tired. She said to herself, "If I can just touch the hem of his garment, I know I'll be made whole." The Bible says that as Jesus was walking by with Jairus, she pressed her way through the crowd even though she was

considered to be unclean. She reached out and touched Jesus and immediately, power went out from Him to her and she was made whole. He turned around and wanted to know who had touched Him. When He looked at the woman who had touched Him, she came and stood before Him scared and shaking. Then she told Him the truth about all that had happened to her and how she had determined in her mind and heart that if she could just get to Him and touch Him, she would be made whole; that she would be healed from the bleeding of her past. Jesus told her that her faith made her whole and declared her to be healed of her infirmity. The scene then switches back to Jairus, a father who had come to Jesus on the behalf of his daughter who he had left at home dying. He told Jesus, "If you just come and lay your hands on my daughter, she will live." Jesus had been on His way to Jairus' house when the bleeding woman touched Him. After He told the woman that she was healed, people came from Jairus' house and said, "There is no hope for your daughter. She is dead." Jesus told Jairus, "Don't be afraid. Just believe." He went to Jairus' house where they were mourning his dead daughter. Jesus told them, "The girl is not dead, she is asleep." and the people laughed. Jesus put the people out and took her father and her mother and three of his disciples into the room with him, shut the door and laid hands on the little girl who was about 12 years old. He said, "Little girl, I say to you, get up." The Bible says the little girl got up and Jesus told them to give her something to eat. *(Mark 5:21-43)*

I tell this story of the sick woman and the dead girl because it's amazing how the two parables are intertwined in the Bible. God showed me that inside of every hurting, bleeding woman is a dead or sleeping little girl. Jesus is able to heal the sick woman and raise up the dead or sleeping little girl on the inside of you. I say to you today, Woman, be healed. Your faith will make you whole! And I say to the little girl that is sleeping or has died on the inside of you, Little girl, get up! Arise. It's time to meet the woman that you have become. It's time to meet the woman that you are today. It's time for the little girl to wake up and connect with the woman who has been healed and made whole! Both the woman with the issue of blood and the father of the little dead girl had to come to Jesus for help. You too must go to God for help. Put your faith and trust in God. Pray to God. Ask God to take away the pain, and He will. Let God heal that hurt that's deep inside of you. It's not over. The little girl in you did not die! God would not let the devil kill her! She was only sleeping!

71

8. **Eat the Word.** You are what you eat. Jesus told them to give the girl something to eat. Sometimes we die not naturally, but spiritually from a lack of spiritual nutrition. I cannot write this book without encouraging you to feed yourself spiritually. It's okay to watch other things on television. I like to watch game shows, Lifetime, and a good movie now and again, but let me encourage you to make sure that you are either watching, listening to, or reading the preached or written Word of God. The Bible says that "Man does not live by bread alone but by every word that comes out of the mouth of God" *(Matthew 4:4)*. We are not only natural beings, but we are also spiritual beings and we have to make sure that we are feeding our spiritual selves just as we feed our natural bodies! Eat the Word. Feast on the Word. Delight yourself in the Word. Edify yourself with the Word of God. Feed your spirit woman so that she can grow strong and overwhelm all of the spiritual attacks that will try to come against you and put you back in bondage to the pain and dysfunction of your past.

9. **Know your value!** You are wonderfully and fearfully made. You are created in the image of God, and that means that you are worthy of honor and respect. Your past, your past experiences or mistakes, anything that you

have done or that has happened to you, or the opinions of other people, do not have the power to validate or invalidate you. God created you, and He is the only own who has the power to give you your true value. You are a one of a kind designer's original, created for great purpose with great power residing on the inside of you. Nothing or no one should be given the power or authority to take that away from you! Refuse to be a people pleaser. Don't play small just to make other people feel better. Do not allow other people's opinions and actions to steal from your value. You are precious, authentic, gifted, talented, beautiful, anointed, intelligent, and powerful. Yes you! Walk in it, and refuse to bow down to any opinion that tries to tear you down from the position of royalty that God has bestowed upon you! You are a woman – you are God's masterpiece. Hold your head up with dignity because when God made you, He broke the mold!

10. **Make the declaration – No more MAN problems!** The words that you release out of your mouth have power. When my youngest daughter was almost two, she was potty training so I took her out of diapers and put her in pullups. She had been struggling with her potty training and still going to the bathroom in her pullups from time to time.

One day I was sitting on the couch, and she came to me with a fresh pullup, the baby wipes, and the powder. Then she laid on the couch, put her legs up and waited for me to change her pullup. I said, "Oh no! If you can do all of that, you can go to the bathroom! No more pullups!" I went and got her some underwear and put them on her. When her father came home from work, she met him at the door and said, "Daddy, no more pullups! No more pullups, Daddy!" And she never needed a pamper or pullup again! She had to get it in her mind and get it out of her mouth that she was free from pullups and able to move forward. We can learn so much from babies! They make up their minds to walk and even if they fall down, they get back up again and keep trying until they walk. They do the same with talking and anything else. We also have to make it up in our minds that we are free from the pain, the mess, and the falling down of our past and get back up and walk. We have to make the declaration of "No more MAN problems!" and even if we stumble and fall, we have to keep getting up and keep making the declaration of "I'm all right! I got this! With God, I can make it! No more bleeding! No more falling! No more anger! No more sadness! No more guilt! No more unforgiveness! No more shame! No more drama! No more relationship issues! No more settling for less! No more MAN problems! No more!"

# CHAPTER 10

## *How Jesus Changed My Life*

I cannot close this book without telling my testimony of how Jesus changed my life. I told you earlier about meeting my husband in the bar and him inviting me to church. I didn't want to go to church because I thought no one in the church was real and that they were all going to Hell with me, and I was sure I was going to Hell; but this dude was persistent and would not stop inviting me to church! I kept avoiding him and even stood him up for a date to go to the movies one time, but one day he got smart and asked me to come to a club in Irvington for Happy Hour.

I met him at the club, and when my friends saw him, they thought he was cute. That got my attention. You know how we sometimes won't really be into a guy until our friends start looking at him thinking he's cute. Well, my attraction level for him went up a few notches with my friend's stamp of approval.

When Anthony came over to me, I was drinking a Long Island Iced Tea. That's a drink with all of the white liquors mixed together and a splash of cola for color. It's a very strong drink and after a long week at work, it was just what the doctor ordered. But there was something about this man that when he came over and started talking to me, made me push my drink away and say, "I don't need to drink anymore of that."

What?!!!

This was coming from a woman who could drink anybody under the table back then.

Then he asked me to dance and after we danced, he asked me had I had anything to eat. I said no and he said, "Come on. Let's go get you something to eat. You don't need to be drinking on an empty stomach."

I remember thinking, *"Yeah, this dude is different. This guy is strange."*

I have had men want to buy me more liquor with hopes of getting me drunk enough to get me to go to bed with them, but I had never met a man who wanted to buy me food to keep me from getting too drunk!

He took me down the street and bought me a couple of pieces of greasy chicken and a rubbery biscuit and as I ate, I remember thinking that was the best chicken and biscuit I had ever had.

God was in that chicken and biscuit! I'm laughing out loud as I type this, but I'm serious. That chicken and biscuit was anointed.

After I ate, we went to sit in my car and Anthony invited me to church again. This time I said I would go. That he could pick me up in the morning.

We said our good nights and I drove off thinking to myself, *"Did I just tell this dude I would go to church with him?"*

The next morning, I got up and pulled the only long dress that I had out of my closet, showered and got ready for church.

When we walked into the church a couple of hours later, I felt like I had come home after being away on a long journey. I felt like I was finally where I belonged.

I went to church with Anthony for the next three months. My boyfriend at the time was in and out of the country on business trips to Africa, and that allowed God plenty of time to use Anthony to draw me to Him. Anthony and I remained friends throughout this process. We hung out all the time until we eventually started dating on the day after Christmas. I gave my life to God on New Year's Eve. It was crazy! We were sitting in the third balcony at The Cathedral a few minutes before midnight, and the preacher said, "If you don't know Jesus, you still have time to come down now and get saved before midnight."

I stood up to go and then I sat back down saying out loud, "No, I'm not going down there. I'm not getting saved."

Then it's like something lifted me back up again. I sat right back down and said, "No. I'm not going!"

The next thing I knew, something lifted me up and took me down the steps and I was standing at the altar with my hands lifted saying the prayer of repentance and faith for salvation! I know now that the something was the Holy Spirit moving me to give my life to the Lord.

That was the beginning of my new life with Jesus Christ. I remember the next day at work and my ex-boyfriend (who had already been moved out of the picture by Anthony but didn't know it) called me from Africa. I told him that I had gotten saved and he said, "What do you mean you got saved?"

I said, "I got saved! I gave my life to the God! I said yes to Jesus!" I was so excited.

I'll never forget his response.

He said, "Uh oh!"

Caught by surprise at his reaction, I asked him, "Uh oh? Why do you say that?"

"Well my dear," he said, "if you said yes to Jesus, that means you say no to me."

I felt like I was in a made for television movie. What was this man talking about? How did he know that I was going to break up with him? I had not even told him yet that we were over. I had not told him that I had met somebody else. Now I realize that this man knew a little bit more about what I had gotten myself into than I did. That was the next to last telephone conversation I had with him and to this day, I have never seen him again. He was right! My saying yes to Jesus meant that he was no longer going to be a part of my life. I did not break up with him verbally that day. I just never got around to seeing him again. The next time he called me from his home in Jersey City to come over late at night, I did not go. I never made another trip to his home – not for the gifts he had brought me from Africa, not for lunch or dinner, and definitely not for another booty call.

I got baptized a month later, and I could feel the Holy Spirit of God all over me. One of the deacons said, "This girl got the Holy Ghost!"

I don't know if I had the Holy Ghost or if the Holy Ghost had me! Either way, I was happy about it! I felt so good, and I could not stop moving! I just kept walking back and forth and praising God.

God totally changed my life from that point on. I was in church every Sunday and in Bible Study every Thursday. There truly is renewal of your mind as you sit under the preached and taught Word of God. God drastically changed my life through His Word and His Holy Spirit!

I began to feel less angry, less bitter, less pain, less shame, and less overall frustration and dissatisfaction with life.

Through the months that followed, I began to trust God more and more and obey the teachings that were coming from the pulpit. I learned to be more kind, to open my heart to love more, and to forgive everyone who had hurt me. At first, I didn't want to forgive, but then God reminded me of how

He had forgiven me of all of the dirty, nasty, horrible things that I had done in my life, and I felt so embarrassed. If God could forgive me of all of that, who was I not to forgive? So, I forgave and forgave and forgave. I forgave the person who molested me. I forgave my father for leaving me. I forgave that young man who stole my virginity and set me up for the gang rape. I forgave my exes for mistreating me and fighting me. I forgave my exes for deceiving me and lying to me. I forgave my ex for cheating on me and sleeping with my cousin (one of the stories I didn't get to tell you). I forgave my ex for hiding that gay porn in the closet. I forgave everyone who had hurt me in life, and then I forgave myself. My God! What a relief that was. I forgave myself for all of the wrong things that I had done in response to all that had been done to me, and God's joy and peace washed over me! I was getting free!

Anthony proposed after a year of dating, and we got married a year after that. We raised his sons from his previous marriage, and had a daughter together. He also helped me with my teenaged daughter who was getting ready to move out at the time that we got married.

We were blessed to buy a house. I wrote my first book and started a publishing company. We were both called to preach and to pastor, and we have been pastoring God's church together for the past 11 years.

God is so good! Over the years, God took away all of my shame, my guilt, my pain and my dysfunction and gave me beauty, joy, peace, love, and blessings in exchange! I am truly a blessed woman, and I know God is not finished blessing and using me for His glory. God gave me a better relationship with my father, my mother, my children, my husband, my brother and sisters, other people, and even with myself. I have been married to my husband for over 22 years and no, everything is not perfect, but nor are things dysfunctional! We are living the God kind of life in a God ordained marriage, and I can truly say that although it is not easy being married and doing all that we do, it is well.

I have no more issues with low self-esteem, anger, bitterness, shame, guilt, people pleasing due to fear of rejection, or looking for love in all the wrong places. I am blessed. My husband is blessed. My children are blessed, and my destiny is blessed.

I told you my story not to brag or boast, but to let you know how awesome God is. I know that I could not have the victory that I have today without giving my life to Jesus. God gets the glory for healing me, delivering me from the pain of my past, present, and future and totally changing my life! Did you get that? God delivered me from all past pain and He continues to deliver me from present and future pain. Pain is inescapable in life. As a matter of fact, I took a major hit in my emotions through something that happened while I was preparing to release this book, but I declare to you that no weapon formed against me has prospered or shall be able to prosper because I have God on my side! The enemy of your destiny did not want me to put this book out. He tried to lie to me and say, "You are not healed. Your life is not that great. How are you going to help somebody else with their life?"

But I told him to "Shut up!"

The devil is a liar and he is already defeated. When you are trying to get free and move forward, there will be opposition, but I challenge you to keep pressing forward towards the goal of being totally healed emotionally and set free from all of the pain of your past and from the MAN problems that have held you back! God gave me the victory even over that recent attack against my emotions and although still in recovery, I declare that the attack has no power over me! God has already given me the victory in every area of my life!

God is no respecter of persons. He does not play favorites. If He did it for me, He can do it for you. If God changed me, He can change anybody! If He healed me, He can heal you too! God is a healer, a deliverer, a provider, a protector, a friend, a doctor, a lawyer, the lifter of our heads, and so much more. Through the redeeming power of the blood of Jesus Christ, I have the victory and you too can have that same story of triumph!

If you know Jesus as your personal Lord and Savior, continue to walk with Him daily as you work out your salvation and emotional healing with fear and trembling. If you do not know Him, let me introduce you to Him.

## The Bible tells it like this:

God so loved the world that He gave His only begotten son to die for us so that whomsoever believes on him should not perish but shall have eternal life with God. *(John 3:16)*

If you confess with your mouth the Lord Jesus Christ and believe in your heart that God raised him from the dead, you shall be saved. For with the heart man believes unto righteousness; and with the mouth confession is made unto salvation. *(Romans 10:9-10)*

Throughout the Bible, we are assured that Jesus, fully God and fully man, took our sins upon himself and died on the cross for our sins. He overpowered death and the grave and got up with all power on the third day. He is now seated on the right hand of God the Father in Heaven.

All you have to do to receive Jesus as personal Lord and Savior and begin to have the supernatural power of the Holy Spirit go to work in your life is to believe, truly believe, in your heart and confess with your mouth that Jesus Christ is Lord and that God raised Him from the dead. God will come to live on the inside of you, and you will be a new creation. All old things from the past that have hindered you will finally be put behind you as are transformed into the image that God originally created you to reflect – His own!

I pray that you believe and receive Jesus Christ as Lord and Savior today. If you decide that you want to, here is a prayer that you can pray:

*Father God, I repent of living my life without you. I believe that you love me so much that you sent your Son, Jesus Christ to die for my sins. I believe in my heart that you raised Jesus from the dead, and I confess with my mouth that Jesus Christ is Lord. Thank you for forgiving all of my sins. Thank you for saving me to have eternal life with you! I pray this prayer in the Name of Jesus.*

If you prayed that prayer from your heart with faith, I welcome you to the family of believers. You are now saved. You are now a Christian. Get into a Bible teaching and preaching church and allow God to transform your life through the renewing of your mind and the power of His Holy Spirit.

## Allow God To Heal You Supernaturally

When you live your life as a Christian, God can supernaturally take away the pain of your past

84

and give you a brand new heart and a brand new life! All of your MAN problems have been put under the blood of Jesus.

What this means is that MAN problems and their side effects have no more authority or power over you. They have been defeated on the cross of Jesus Christ. You have been given authority as a believer, and you have the power to begin to speak wholeness and healing over your life and have it manifest because of the authority that has been given to you. You have the power to war in the supernatural realm over your future through prayer, praise, worship, and the words that you speak out of your mouth. You have the victory over MAN problems through the power of the Holy Spirit and the prophetic promises of God contained in His Word in the Bible.

Learn the Word of God. Learn God's promises. Cultivate a personal relationship with God through prayer, reading your Bible, and praise and worship. Ask God to take away the pain, the shame, the misplaced guilt and other negative emotions, the bad habits, and any behavior that you want to stop, and watch Him do it.

You are positioned for guaranteed, manifested victory! No weapon formed against you, even the past issues wrapped up in MAN problems, shall prosper in your life! Nothing shall be able to triumph over you! You have the victory in the Name of Jesus! In the Name of Jesus, you have the victory! Hallelujah! To God be the glory!

# CHAPTER 11

## *Moving Forward From MAN Problems To Power*

God has a great plan for your life. He has a plan to prosper you and not to harm you. God has a plan to give you hope for your future. He has a plan for your happiness. God has a plan for your success. You don't have to live a life of looking for love in all the wrong places. You don't have to wake up looking in all the wrong faces. You don't have to get drunk, do drugs, engage in sexual behavior that brings you shame, or put up with a relationship with someone who is not worthy of being in relationship with you or who is not that into you. You are worthy of the love of a good man. You don't have to be a side chick or a jump off! You are not somebody's whore or what they want to call a THOT! (That Hoe Over There).

You are a woman of great value, intellect, beauty and potential. You are already precious. You don't need anyone's stamp of approval on you. You don't need someone to validate or complete you. God created you as a designer's original. When God made you, He broke the mold.

You are the only one that could be you. There is no one exactly like you. You are awesome in your own original identity! Embrace it!

What the devil meant for evil when he brought all of those roadblocks, barriers, problems, and negative emotions into your life as a child or even through your adult years, God is turning that thing around for your good. What was meant to destroy you, could not do the job! You survived the attack and came out alive. You came out on top! The fact that you are still here shows that you were meant to survive!

I always say the devil should have killed me when he had a chance. Yes, I picked up the drugs and the alcohol, slept with the men and diluted my own value due to my issues, due to my MAN problems, but once I got free, I got free for real and I will no longer be bound by the things that held me down in the past. I want you to make that same confession and declaration. You have survived what was meant to take you out and what has destroyed so many other women. You are not just a survivor, you are more than a conqueror! You are victorious! You are awesome!

So, as I prepare to close out this book, I thank God for you and *your* testimony. I thank God for your breakthrough and your victory. I encourage you to take the action steps that I have outlined to overcome molestation, harmful negative experiences, sex against your will, and for resolving MAN problems. Some of them are repetitive, but just like the blind man in the Bible, sometimes we need a repeat touch in order to get our total sight back or our total healing. *(Mark 8:23-25)*

I challenge you not to skip over any of the action steps and to read through this entire book. What you think might not be for you, may well be for you. At least you'll get to hear some interesting testimonies of parts of my life story and be encouraged by my experiences. You don't have to walk alone. I challenge you if you are feeling stuck, to reach out and get some help in dealing with the issues that have held you bound for so long. I declare today that if you keep moving forward in your endeavor to be free, that you will be free! There are organizations for molested and sexually assaulted women like RAINN, also there are psychologists, counsellors, and clergy that can walk through your journey of healing with you. You can get more information about RAINN by going to www.RAINN.org.

I challenge you to leave the past in the past, and press forward to the glorious future that awaits you. Your worst days are behind you, better is here, and the best is yet to come. God has so much more in store for you. Your eyes have not seen, nor have your ears heard, neither has it entered into your heart or mind the things that God has in store for you. Get ready for your unstoppable destiny. Get ready for more joy. Get ready for more peace. Get ready for more power.

Get ready for more. Get ready for better in your relationships. Get ready for better in your marriage. Get ready for better with your children. Get ready for better.

## *My Prayer For You*

*Father God, I thank you for my sister reading this book right now. I praise you and magnify your Name. Lord, you are awesome, and I love you so much. I lift up my sister to you and ask Lord that you allow this book to be an instrument of healing in her life. I ask that not one word that she reads will fall to the ground or come back void.*

*I ask you to touch her afresh and anew and that you would heal her right now of any MAN problems or any residue from MAN problems that may be impacting her life. I ask that you take away the pain of her past and make her whole. Allow her to walk forward in victory today and every day for the rest of her life. I ask that you bring her beauty for ashes and joy for mourning. I ask that you give her a garment of praise in replacement of any spirit of heaviness.*

*I ask that you anoint her body, her mind, and her eyes and give her the spiritual vision to see all that you have ordained for her. Lord, I touch and agree with her and bind up the hand of the enemy and cancel all of his plans for her life, and I loose the power of the blood of Jesus that gives her the victory! Lord thank you for healing us and bringing us out of darkness into your marvelous light. I thank you for my sister. I thank you for her life. I thank you for her healing. I thank you for her victory, and I declare it to be so. It's in the Name of Jesus that I pray this prayer, and I and my sister say, Amen.*

## Move Forward In Victory With Prayer

I challenge you to move forward in victory with a lifestyle of prayer. Prayer will help you to make it when the enemy tries to enter your mind and pull you back into a state of pain, guilt, shame and dysfunction. Prayer will be your compass to let you know what steps to take and what decisions to make. God, through prayer will heal you, strengthen you, encourage you, enlighten you, empower you and equip you to keep fighting and winning life's battles. The Bible tells us to pray without ceasing. Prayer is your power connection that keeps you walking in close relationship with God.

Commit to spend some time every morning and every night in prayer. When you feel sad, pray. When you feel like quitting, pray. When you feel like falling back into old habits or going back to old dysfunctional relationships, pray! God will keep you on the right path. He will steer you in the direction of your blessings and your destiny. He will show you who to connect with and who to run from.

Prayer is necessary. It is how we communicate with God. Prayer is powerful. It is a weapon! Use it and use it often. God is a very present help in the time of trouble. Prayer is how we get God involved in our healing and in our lives. Prayer truly does change things. So, I challenge you to pray and then go ahead and praise God for the manifestation of what you have prayed for. Praise God for wholeness. Praise God for healing. Praise God for relationships that bring you joy and laughter instead of tears. Praise God for hope for your future. Praise God for your breakthrough!

## Take Care of Yourself As You Move Forward

Take good care of yourself. No matter how other people act towards you, treat yourself like the queen that you are. I have talked to many women and even wives who are stressing out over the men in their lives. Most of them have lost themselves in that boyfriend or that husband. They have literally lost their own identity and are living their lives wrapped up in a man. We have to be careful not to give our God given identity away to someone else. You were born into this earth because God has a very specific plan for your life. What happened to you in the past came to steal, kill, and destroy that plan, but you have to be determined to live the life that you were born to live. You have to be determined to live your life in such a way that your light is shining and your purpose is fulfilled.

## Steps To Taking Care of Yourself:

1. **Love yourself enough.** You must love yourself enough to be the best you that you can be. Eat the right foods, exercise on a regular basis, Take care of your health by getting your annual checkup and exams. Don't let yourself go by using food for comfort and overeating, not sleeping, and neglecting your personal self-care. Pamper yourself by getting your hair and nails done and buying the occasional new outfit. Commit to love God, love yourself, and then extend love out to others.

2. **Find and pursue your passion.** What is that thing that you are really passionate about that you have been putting off because you didn't have enough self-esteem or motivation to pursue it? A large part of your purpose is your passion. Take your focus off of other people, your man, or even your husband and focus on something the you have always wanted to do that would bring you joy. Get out of the house, and get your life! Take up a hobby, go on a trip, go back to school, or start a new career! There are so many options to explore. Get out of your own way, and get out there and live.

3. **Don't let anyone take your joy!** The only way to do this is to realign your focus. You can no

longer afford to focus on them and what they did or are doing. Keep your focus on God and what He has done in bringing you to a place of healing and restoration. If you find yourself getting depressed because of the past or someone that you are in a relationship with or married to, shift your attention back to the blessings that you currently have in your life. Pray, put on some music and dance or praise God, or take yourself out to dinner. Whatever you do, don't give away your joy!

4. **Daily re-affirm your healing and victory.** Use the affirmations in the next chapter to speak positive, victorious words over your life everyday.


God's plan for victory shall come to pass in your life. No weapon formed against you, past, present or future is going to prosper. You are already more than a conqueror over everything that has tried to conquer and imprison you. You have the victory! Refuse to let the enemy hold you back. Refuse to stay stuck in the past any longer. Pay no more attention to those things behind you, but press forward for the prize that God has set before you! Keep pressing! Keep moving forward. Don't settle for less. Keep believing for the best in life. Keep believing for the best in your relationships or your marriage. It's possible! With God, all things are possible!

# CHAPTER 12

## *Daily Affirmations For Power*

**Read through these affirmations every day! As time goes by, highlight the ones that speak to you and declare them out loud each and every day.**

1. I am wonderfully and fearfully made.

2. I am not responsible for other people's bad behavior towards me.

3. I don't need people to validate me. God's Word tells me that I am special.

4. I am moving forward to the abundant life that God has promised me.

5. I am not a victim of my circumstances.

6. I love me.

7. I am happy being the person that I am today while pressing to be an even better me tomorrow.

8. I do not need sex, drugs, or alcohol to make me feel good or to help me deal with problems that I have in my life.

9. I am more than a conqueror through Jesus Christ.

10. There is no weapon formed against me, past or present that can prosper or destroy me.

11. I choose to forgive the people who hurt me so that I can go on to live a blessed life.

12. I know that trials and tribulations in this life will only make me better.

13. I am striving daily to be the best me possible.

14. Today is the first day of the rest of my life.

15. I will only surround myself with positive, faith-filled people.

16. I am a child of God, and God cares about me.

17. I was born to win.

18. I deserve the best in relationships and love, and I will not settle for less.

19. I am created in the image of God.

20. I am worthy of honor and respect.

21. My past experiences and mistakes do not take away from my value.

22. I have the power of God working in me.

23. I have been forgiven by God of my past mistakes.

24. God has a great plan for my life.

25. God has a plan to prosper me and not to harm me.

26. God has a plan to give me hope for my future.

27. Yesterday ended last night. Today is the first day of the rest of my life.

28. I have already been given victory through the shed blood of Jesus Christ.

29. I cast out guilt and shame. I am not under condemnation for my past.

30. Things that happened to me are not my fault and I choose not to live my life as a victim.

31. I forgive everyone who has hurt me because I refuse to be bound by anger and bitterness.

32. I choose to love even my enemies.

33. I will only allow myself to be in relationships that honor and respect my value.

34. I am valuable. I am more precious than diamonds, pearls, and rubies.

35. God loves me. I love me. I am blessed to be me!

# ABOUT THE AUTHOR

*Rebecca Simmons aka Pastor Rebecca* is a power-filled prophetic preacher! She is a wife who loves her husband. She and her husband have been married for 21 years. They have four children and four grandchildren. She is a mother and grandmother who loves and nurtures her children and grandchildren. She pastors New Creation Christian Ministries with her husband. She is also the owner of Diligence Publishing Company where she helps authors to write and publish Kingdom ordained books.

She is a powerful preacher with a testimony that God is using for His glory. She ministers deliverance through the power of the Holy Spirit and is courageous when it comes to spiritual warfare. She is a virtuous woman who has seen God work in her own life as well as the life of her husband. She became a born-again Christian in 1994 and received the call to preach in 2002. She and her husband founded New Creation Christian Ministries in 2006 where they faithfully serve the people that God sends to the church. She has been used by God to write a motivational book, two healing, evangelistic novels, a marriage book, and a healing inspirational book for women. Pastor Rebecca hosts a weekly live broadcast "Woman to Woman With Pastor Rebecca." You can tune in by connecting to the

Woman To Woman With Pastor Rebecca page on Facebook.

Pastor Rebecca is the visionary and founder of Woman To Woman Empowerment Group on Facebook. You can join by connecting with Pastor Rebecca on Facebook.

Pastor Rebecca's church website is: http://www.nccmonline.org.

Her book titles are *Nobody's Business, Daddy Love, The Cry of a Woman's Heart; Healing the Pain of the Past, Traveling the Road to Victorious Living, Pump Up The Power: Get The Life You Want, Don't Die In The Wilderness,* and *Making Marriage and Relationships Work.* These books are available at http://www.dpc-books.com, Amazon.com, and by request at your local bookstore.

The author would love to have you connect with her on Facebook and Twitter.

# ORDER INFORMATION

You can order additional copies of MAN PROBLEMS at your local bookstore and distributors or by emailing the author directly using the email address below.

Rebecca Simmons

Email Address: powerintheword1@yahoo.com

Please leave a review for this book on Amazon and let other readers know how much you enjoyed reading it.

Thank you!

Made in the USA
Middletown, DE
16 January 2018